NO GOOD DEED GOES UNPUNISHED

A one-act comedy by
Cheryl Hadley

www.youthplays.com
info@youthplays.com
424-703-5315

COPYRIGHT RULES TO REMEMBER

CAST OF CHARACTERS

WIDGINA, a kind, level-headed girl who narrates her own story.

SQUIRE, the put-upon servant of the Prince.

YOUNG WIDGINA, the Widgina (or Widginas) acting out the story.

PRINCE, a three-timing, not-too-bright young man.

RAPUNZEL, she of the long hair (and feather brain).

SNOW WHITE, a rambunctious, young princess.

CINDERELLA, nice enough; looking for her prince.

STRAW-INTO-GOLD MAIDEN, slave to Rumplestiltskin.

GRANNY, Red Riding Hood's slave driver grandmother.

RUMPLESTILTSKIN, local realtor and gold lover.

KING, Snow White's father.

MAGIC MIRROR, a voice from offstage.

HANSEL & GRETEL, two mischievous (and hungry) children.

RED RIDING HOOD, helps her Granny clean houses (while not eating snacks).

RAPUNZEL'S MOTHER, off her rocker; the type who would leave a baby at the neighbor's and forget.

DWARF BROTHERS, messy, party-throwing imps.

HANSEL & GRETEL'S PARENTS, worried about their children.

ANGRY MOB, pretty much how that sounds.

SCENE 1

(A bench in the middle of the woods. A street sign shows various locations and their directions and distances. WIDGINA, bag in hand, is in a hurry, looking behind her as she enters.)

WIDGINA: *(To audience:)* I think I've finally lost them! You know what they say about no good deed going unpunished? Well, it's true. Trust me!

(She plops down on the bench and drops her bag on the ground. She pulls off one shoe and rubs her foot.)

Oh, my aching feet! These shoes weren't exactly made for running!

(She holds up the clunky heel.)

I really need to remember to keep the Dr. Scholl's by the door! I wonder if there's a Haunted Forest Foot Locker around somewhere?

(She takes out a mirror.)

Ahh! I look a fright!

(HANSEL and GRETEL enter, leading an ANGRY MOB. Widgina notices, grabs her bag and hides behind a tree.)

GRETEL: I think she went this way!

HANSEL: No, she went that way. I think I see her cloak!

MOB: This way!
No, that way!
I'm confused! Which way?
Well, why didn't ya say so?

(As Hansel and Gretel argue, the Mob becomes more exasperated. The SQUIRE emerges from the crowd and pops up

behind Widgina. Just as she is about to scream, he puts his hand over her mouth and gestures her to stay hidden.)

SQUIRE: *(Shouting and pointing SL:)* She went that way!

MOB: Yeah! That way!
Wasn't it this way?
I'm even more confused!
Well, why didn't ya say so?

SQUIRE: *(Looking both ways:)* You can come out now. They're gone.

WIDGINA: *(Plopping onto bench:)* That was close! Thanks.

SQUIRE: You're welcome. So, Witch, now maybe you can help me out!

WIDGINA: *(Stupefied:)* What did you call me?

SQUIRE: Oh, I'm sorry—do you prefer "wiccans" these days? I apologize. It's so hard to keep up with the correct terminology...

WIDGINA: *(Still stupefied:)* What in the world makes you think I'm a witch?

SQUIRE: So it IS witch! Now I have to admit, I'm a bit confused...

WIDGINA: No, no! I'm not a witch! Where did you get that idea, anyway?

SQUIRE: *(Giving a look to the audience:)* Um, have you taken a look at yourself lately?

(He hands Widgina a mirror. She takes the mirror and looks at herself. She pulls a cobweb from her hair and continues to try to make herself more presentable.)

WIDGINA: Oh! Okay, well, I guess I don't exactly look like I'm on the way to the Prince's Ball, but I've had a horrible day! I was just forced to leave my home and chased through the forest by an angry mob!

(She straightens herself up a bit.)

Still, I don't think my...unusual appearance warrants you calling me a witch!

SQUIRE: Well, how about dozens of people chasing you, shouting, "Witch!"?

WIDGINA: *(Thinking:)* I guess that might do it...

SQUIRE: So, since I saved you, when do I get my three wishes?

WIDGINA: What? That's not even a witch! That's a genie!

SQUIRE: My pot of gold?

WIDGINA: That's a leprechaun!

SQUIRE: My...lottery ticket?

WIDGINA: Okay, let's stop this!! I am not a witch! So the most I can do is give you this.

(She hands him a gingerbread cookie.)

SQUIRE: A cookie? That's the best you've got?

WIDGINA: Again! I was in a hurry! *(To audience:)* This guy's pretty thick.

SQUIRE: *(Pauses)* So you're sure you're not a witch?

WIDGINA: Positive!

SQUIRE: Then why do you wear your hair like that?

WIDGINA: *(Trying again to make herself more presentable:)* It's a long story.

SQUIRE: *(Looking around:)* Well, if I'm not getting any wishes out of this, I have time.

WIDGINA: Well, it has to do with my first good deed gone awry. See, I have a habit of getting into these situations that don't turn out very well.

SCENE 2

(Lights darken as Widgina continues her story. Lights come up on garden and cottage. Young Widgina 1 enters the garden.)

WIDGINA: It all started when I was very young—not more than fifteen.

SQUIRE: *(Looking at Young Widgina:)* Hey! That doesn't look like you! She's way taller! And she has dark hair!

WIDGINA: It's called literary license! Now, my parents had died with the fever when I was younger.

SQUIRE: Oh, that's terrible! What kind of fever?

(Widgina looks to audience, shrugs her shoulders, and then looks back at the Squire.)

WIDGINA: What kind of fever? I don't know, Disco Fever! It was The Fever! Can I continue?

SQUIRE: *(Rattled:)* Sorry. Um, sure. *(To audience:)* Yeah, she's not a witch!

(GRANNY joins Young Widgina in the garden.)

WIDGINA: Since my parents died when I was so young, I was raised by my Granny. We lived a quiet life on the outskirts of the village. We had a small cottage, but Granny raised a beautiful garden.

SQUIRE: What did you grow?

(Widgina looks to audience, then shoots a dirty look to the Squire. He cowers.)

WIDGINA: Well, Granny had gone to visit her sister in the next village.

(RAPUNZEL'S MOTHER enters carrying a baby and acting crazy. She sets the baby down and starts eating items from the garden.)

YOUNG WIDGINA: *(Noticing Rapunzel's Mother in the garden:)* Oh, hello! Can I help you?

RAPUNZEL'S MOTHER: *(With her mouth full:)* No, no! Just passing through! Gotta go!

(Rapunzel's Mother runs through the garden, picking more vegetables as she goes. Young Widgina notices that she left the baby.)

YOUNG WIDGINA: Hey, wait! You forgot your baby!

(Rapunzel's Mother leaves without hearing her.)

What am I supposed to do now?

(She picks up the baby and walks around the garden.)

SQUIRE: So what did you do?

WIDGINA: Well, what could I do? I took the baby to the cottage. A beautiful baby girl! I assumed her mother would return for her.

SQUIRE: Did she?

WIDGINA: Not for a very long time. So when Granny came back from her sister's, we raised the child like one of our own. Granny named her Rapunzel. She was kind of lazy, and not too bright.

SCENE 3

(The garden, years later. RAPUNZEL is a young girl. She and YOUNG WIDGINA 1 are working in the garden.)

YOUNG WIDGINA : Rapunzel, Rapunzel! It's the red ones that are ripe!

RAPUNZEL: *(Plopping down in front of the garden:)* Oh, I can't remember this. Red, green—it's all the same to me. I really can't be bothered with such things.

YOUNG WIDGINA: But it's not that hard! Red—ripe! Green—wait!

RAPUNZEL: But there are so many more important things in the world to worry about!

YOUNG WIDGINA: Like what?

RAPUNZEL: Well... *(Staring at the sky:)* ...my hair, for one thing!

(She looks at her hair.)

YOUNG WIDGINA: Come on, Rapunzel. Help me finish up here so we can go eat.

RAPUNZEL: *(Noticing a knot in her hair:)* AUGH!

YOUNG WIDGINA: What's wrong?

RAPUNZEL: My hair! It has a knot!

(Rapunzel runs into the house.)

I need a brush right away!

(She reappears in the window.)

(Young Widgina continues to pick vegetables while Rapunzel brushes her hair in the window. A PRINCE walks into the garden and immediately notices Rapunzel's beauty.)

PRINCE: Oh, what rapturous beauty is this? Were she a rose, she could not be more beautiful! Were she a star, she could not be more radiant! Pray, young maiden, what is your name?

RAPUNZEL: *(At first startled, then giggling:)* Rapunzel!

PRINCE: What a delightfully melodic name!

(Rapunzel giggles.)

My rare and precious flower—come from your humble cottage and let me kiss your hand!

(Rapunzel giggles.)

YOUNG WIDGINA: Rapunzel, what are you doing?

RAPUNZEL: *(Startled by Young Widgina, to Prince:)* Oh, no! You'd better go! If she finds me talking with you... *(Turning to audience:)* ...and not picking the vegetables... *(Turns back to Prince:)* ...she'll be so mad!

PRINCE: Who could dare be angry with such a delicate creature as yourself?

RAPUNZEL: Witchie.

PRINCE: *(To himself:)* A witch! Curses! *(To Rapunzel:)* Be patient, young maiden. I shall return with a plan!

(He exits.)

RAPUNZEL: Wait! A plan for what? Wait! Oh, darn.

YOUNG WIDGINA: Rapunzel! Did you finish your part of the garden?

RAPUNZEL: *(Running out to meet Young Widgina:)* Um, almost.

YOUNG WIDGINA: You've barely done anything! *(Sighing:)* Oh, well. Let's get to work.

(Lights go out on garden. Lights go up on Widgina and the Squire.)

SQUIRE: So far this story isn't so bad. But I couldn't help but notice...that she called you a WITCH!

WIDGINA: No, no, no! That's what everyone thinks! She called me "Witchie."

SQUIRE: *(Pause.)* Is that somehow supposed to be less offensive?

WIDGINA: *(Looking at audience with distaste:)* You see, my name is Widgina. Rapunzel could never say it right when she was little, so it always came out "Witchie."

SQUIRE: I guess it does sound sort of similar. I can see how the Prince was mistaken.

WIDGINA: Oh, the Prince was an idiot!

SQUIRE: Tell me what happened.

WIDGINA: The Prince decided he had to save Rapunzel from the "evil witch," so he devised a plan.

(Lights dim on Widgina and Squire. Lights go up on the cottage scene. The Prince and Rapunzel are talking at the window.)

Like I said, the Prince was pretty dim. He kept coming around to see Rapunzel. He'd tell her stories about his kingdom, and Rapunzel would giggle through the window at him. Every time I came near, the Prince would run away.

(Young Widgina approaches and the Prince exits.)

YOUNG WIDGINA: Rapunzel, why does he keep doing that?

RAPUNZEL: I don't know. Oh, isn't he cute?

YOUNG WIDGINA: He's cute, all right, but he makes me nervous.

(Lights go up on Widgina and Squire.)

WIDGINA: Then one day everything went crazy! I came back early one day and found the strange woman had finally returned to the garden.

(Rapunzel's Mother enters the garden, looking a little crazy:)

RAPUNZEL'S MOTHER: Oh! I feel like I've been here before.

(Prince enters the other side of the garden.)

PRINCE: Rapunzel! Rapunzel! Let thou appear!

(Rapunzel comes to the window.)

Come, my beauty! Let us leave this wretched place. I will steal you away before the horrible witch returns!

RAPUNZEL AND RAPUNZEL'S MOTHER: Witch?!

(The Prince paces nervously in front of the cottage, looking offstage frequently.)

RAPUNZEL'S MOTHER: That's it! Now I remember! I...I was in this garden before! Yes! The...the witch's garden! I ate some...enchanted vegetables! Yes! And they took away my memory! That must be it!

(She looks horrified as she runs hurriedly offstage.)

My baby! Yes, the witch took away my baby! My baby, my baby!

PRINCE: Hurry, my love! She approaches!

RAPUNZEL: Um, who approaches?

PRINCE: The witch!

(Widgina enters stage right, as a CROWD of villagers enters stage left. The Prince grabs Rapunzel by the hair and pulls her out the window, pointing at Young Widgina.)

The witch! She's here!

CROWD: The witch! The witch!
Where's a witch?
I didn't know about any witch!
Well, why didn't you say so?

> *(The Crowd starts running after Young Widgina, who drops her basket in surprise and runs off. Lights go down on cottage. Lights go up on Widgina and Squire.)*

SQUIRE: So what happened next? Did Rapunzel marry the Prince? Did the woman find out she was Rapunzel's mother?

WIDGINA: Enough already with all the questions!

SQUIRE: Well, tell me!

WIDGINA: I can't.

SQUIRE: What? Why not?

WIDGINA: I just can't.

SQUIRE: WHY NOT?

WIDGINA: Because I don't know! I never went back there again.

SQUIRE: What?!

WIDGINA: The villagers chased me, yelling, "Witch! Witch!" all through the forest. It was all I could do to get away.

SQUIRE: Why didn't you just explain?

WIDGINA: Some of those people were carrying pitchforks! Have you ever been stabbed with a pitchfork?

SQUIRE: Well, surely Rapunzel could have explained.

WIDGINA: That would have been great, wouldn't it? But I imagine Rapunzel was too busy giggling at the Prince to help. *(To audience:)* I mean, did you see the head of hair on that girl? *(Pointing to her head:)* I think that was all she had going on up there!

SCENE 4

(The forest. Young Widgina 2 enters out of breath.)

WIDGINA: But once I lost the villagers, I noticed how interesting the forest was. And it was full of interesting people.

SQUIRE: Hey! She looks completely different!

WIDGINA: Give me a break. Haven't you heard of child labor laws?

(RED RIDING HOOD and DWARVES go past Young Widgina as she walks through the forest.)

I'd never been further than the village, and I'd never really done anything except tend the garden and take care of Rapunzel. Now that I was in this fascinating new place, I never went back to the cottage.

(Squire shakes his head in shame.)

Hey, she had the Prince! She didn't need me.

SQUIRE: Well, what happened next?

WIDGINA: I had to find a place to live. And a job, of course. That was when I met Granny, and she gave me a job.

(Granny enters the forest and talks with Young Widgina.)

SQUIRE: *(Confused:)* YOUR Granny?

WIDGINA: No, of course not MY Granny. Remember — this is a fairy tale. Every old woman is Granny!

SQUIRE: *(Looking at Granny:)* But she looks an awful lot like your Granny!

WIDGINA: *(To audience:)* What can I say? We've got a budget!

SQUIRE: Oh, go on!

WIDGINA: Thank you.

GRANNY: Well, who do we have here?

YOUNG WIDGINA: *(With a curtsy:)* Widgina, ma'am! How do you do?

GRANNY: Don't you look a sight! Whatcha been doin'? Runnin' through the forest at night?

YOUNG WIDGINA: *(Looking at herself:)* Yeah, that's about it.

GRANNY: You look like someone in need of a place to stay.

(Young Widgina nods.)

Well, you just come with me. Granny runs a cleaning service, and I can always use another body to clean houses.

(Lights up on Widgina and Squire.)

SQUIRE: Well, that was nice of her!

WIDGINA: That's what I thought at first, too. But Granny was a real wolf when it came to work!

GRANNY: You can stay with me, dearie!

WIDGINA: Oh, thank you, Granny. How can I ever repay you?

GRANNY: Well, sweetie, you can just clean a few houses for me. *(To audience:)* For the rest of your life!

SQUIRE: What did she mean by that?

WIDGINA: Granny kept tabs on everything. What I ate. What I drank. She even charged rent on the pillow I used! Soon I was so far in debt to Granny that I was working day and night cleaning houses to pay her back.

(Red enters.)

RED: Do you want a muffin? Or maybe a fresh-baked cookie? Granny just made them special!

(She waves her basket in front of Young Widgina's nose.)

YOUNG WIDGINA: *(Resisting:)* No! I can't work forever for cookies!

RED: You're right!   Who needs cookies?   Hot, ooey-gooey chocolate chip cookies!

(Red waves a cookie at Young Widgina, then takes a bite.)

YOUNG WIDGINA: *(Giving in:)* Okay, okay. But just one! *(Taking a cookie:)* Mmm!

RED: Granny needs you to go clean the Dwarf Brothers' house.

YOUNG WIDGINA: The Dwarf Brothers' house?

RED: Yep! And I hear they had a party last night! Ta-ta!

(Red skips away. Lights out on forest.)

SQUIRE: Who were the Dwarf Brothers?

WIDGINA: Just the dirtiest, filthiest little people in the whole forest!

SQUIRE: How many were there? *(To audience:)* Just curious!

WIDGINA: Well, no one really ever knew for sure. They were really small and very fast, and they all looked alike! There might have been two or three, or maybe as many as seven. They never stayed in one place long enough for anyone to count them!

SCENE 5

(Outside the Dwarf Brothers' cave. We don't really see the cave, only outside. Young Widgina approaches.)

(Lights up on scene. Young Widgina approaches the cave.)

YOUNG WIDGINA: *(Calling in:)* Anybody home? I'm from Granny's cleaning service! I'm here to clean up after your party!

(Some Dwarves come out and pull Young Widgina offstage, into the cave. Shrieks are heard from Young Widgina, then cries of disgust, followed by sounds of cleaning.)

SQUIRE: Shouldn't we try to help her? *(A little confused:)* I mean...you?

WIDGINA: No, she'll be okay. I mean, I was okay. The Dwarf Brothers were very messy, but not mean— *(To audience:)* —just a little grumpy!

SQUIRE: So what happened?

WIDGINA: I finished cleaning and headed back to Granny's.

YOUNG WIDGINA: Maybe you should consider not serving Cheese Whiz at your next party!

DWARF 1: *(Paying Young Widgina:)* Just tell Granny there will be another party next week!

(Young Widgina walks through the forest and runs into SNOW WHITE, sitting on the ground, crying.)

YOUNG WIDGINA: Oh, dear! What's wrong?

SNOW WHITE: I'm running away.

YOUNG WIDGINA: Running away? From what?

SNOW WHITE: Not a what—a who! My father is so unreasonable!

YOUNG WIDGINA: Well, running away isn't the answer.

SQUIRE: Look who's talking!

WIDGINA: Shhh!

YOUNG WIDGINA: Why don't I walk you back home? We can talk about it on the way.

(They start walking.)

SNOW WHITE: I guess. Well, I wanted to go out to the Dwarf Brothers' party last night, but Daddy said I wasn't old enough. I mean, really, I'm almost fifteen! What is he thinking? All my friends get to go out whenever they want!

YOUNG WIDGINA: Well, I'm sure it's because he loves you so much.

SNOW WHITE: I suppose it's because he lost Momma so young. I guess I can't really blame him for wanting to keep me close.

(KING enters from offstage.)

KING: Snow White! *(Rushing to hug her:)* I've been looking everywhere for you!

SNOW WHITE: Oh, Daddy! I'm sorry! Oh, I almost forgot. Daddy, this is...um, I don't think I got your name!

YOUNG WIDGINA: Widgina.

SNOW WHITE: *(Scrunching up her face:)* Really?

YOUNG WIDGINA: Really.

SNOW WHITE: Um, I think I'll call you Bubbles! Daddy, this is Bubbles. She found me and walked with me the whole way here! She's so great.

KING: *(To Young Widgina:)* How do you do? You have my

sincerest gratitude.

SNOW WHITE: Can't Bubbles come and stay with us, Daddy? I need someone to talk to and, after all, the castle could use another woman's touch!

KING: Well, I don't know. Miss...uh, Bubbles may have other plans, dear.

SNOW WHITE: I don't care! I want her!

KING: All right, dear, calm down. We'll see what we can do. Miss Bubbles, would you be willing to move to the castle and be Snow White's companion?

YOUNG WIDGINA: Well, I have obligations to Granny.

KING: Not another word. I have had dealings with Granny. Consider your debt to her paid. When you go and get your belongings, simply tell her to see my court treasurer.

(Lights out on forest.)

SQUIRE: So you didn't have to clean houses anymore.

WIDGINA: I wouldn't say that. I had to clean up after Snow White! She was sweet, but she was a wild child! I constantly had to be on my toes. She would sneak out at least once a week!

SQUIRE: That sounds like a pain.

WIDGINA: It was, but I had a secret weapon. The King had a Magic Mirror that would show me where Snow White was every minute.

SQUIRE: That seems invasive!

WIDGINA: I only used it when it was really necessary.

SQUIRE: How often was that?

WIDGINA: A couple times a week.

SCENE 6

(Lights up on room with MAGIC MIRROR. Young Widgina is in a black cloak with a witch mask.)

SQUIRE: *(Seeing the witch get-up:)* Ahh! What happened to her? You?

WIDGINA: Oh, I was dressed up for a party.

SQUIRE: That must have been some party!

WIDGINA: It was a spooky fair for the kids in the kingdom. But my new job was to attend to Snow White first, so she took priority. I was pretty angry with her.

YOUNG WIDGINA: I can't believe Snow White did this again today! She knew how important it was for me to be at the fair on time. I suppose she's over at the Dwarf Brothers' house again. I'd better check to make sure. "Mirror, Mirror, on the wall, Where has Snow White gone to call?"

MAGIC MIRROR: Snow White has run off to the Dwarf Brothers' again, my lady. It looks like they're having a wild party.

YOUNG WIDGINA: Oh, it looks like I just have enough time to get to her before the fair.

MAGIC MIRROR: For once, why don't you just leave her to face her own consequences?

YOUNG WIDGINA: I think I'd lose my job and my place to stay. Besides, she really is a good girl—just misguided.

MAGIC MIRROR: Good luck! Better hurry—oh, and don't forget your apples!

YOUNG WIDGINA: Thanks.

(Lights out on Magic Mirror.)

SQUIRE: So you actually went out looking like that?

WIDGINA: Well, I was in a hurry.

SCENE 7

(Outside the Dwarf Brothers' cave.   Young Widgina approaches.)

YOUNG WIDGINA: *(Calling in:)* Come on, princess! We have to go!

SNOW WHITE: You're no fun! I don't want to leave. There's a really cute prince coming! Please, stay with me. Daddy won't mind if you're here with me. Please, you... *(Seeing Young Widgina in mask:)* AAHHH!

YOUNG WIDGINA: *(Taking mask off:)* Shh! It's just me!

SNOW WHITE: Oh! Why are you wearing that? I mean, it's not very attractive. Do you really think you're going to find a man looking like that? I mean, come on, you're...

YOUNG WIDGINA: I'm going to be late!

SNOW WHITE: Oh, those kids won't care. They don't need you as much as I do. The Prince will be here soon, and...

YOUNG WIDGINA: *(To audience:)* Maybe this will shut her up for a while!

(She hands Snow White an apple.)

SNOW WHITE: Oh, thank you!

(She eats the apple and continues to talk.)

I was getting pretty hungry. The Dwarf Brothers never have any good food around...

(Snow White starts to choke. She holds her neck.)

YOUNG WIDGINA: Oh, no! Can you talk?

(Snow White shakes her head.)

SQUIRE: You finally rendered her speechless!

WIDGINA: It wasn't exactly my plan.

(Young Widgina starts performing the Heimlich maneuver on Snow White. Prince arrives from stage left just as the Dwarf Brothers arrive from stage right.)

PRINCE: You there! What are you doing? Unhand that fair young princess!

SQUIRE: Hey, isn't that the same Prince who ran away with Rapunzel?

WIDGINA: I don't know. One prince pretty much looks like another to me.

PRINCE: I said unhand that princess!

(Young Widgina looks up at the Prince. Snow White spits the apple out of her mouth. The Dwarf Brothers look at Young Widgina.)

PRINCE & DWARF BROTHERS: *(Screaming:)* Witch!!

(Young Widgina drops an exhausted Snow White to the ground as the Prince and Dwarf Brothers yell.)

PRINCE: I shall show you, witch, what happens when you try to harm a lovely maid such as this!

(He pulls out sword.)

SNOW WHITE: *(Panting:)* But...she's...

PRINCE: Hush, my love!

(He rushes to her side. He calls to Dwarf Brothers.)

After her!

(Dwarf Brothers and Angry Mob loudly chase Young Widgina offstage.)

MOB: This way!

No, that way!
I'm confused! Which way?
Well, why didn't ya say so?

SQUIRE: There seems to be a pattern here...

   (Widgina gives Squire a dirty look.)

So you just left Snow White there?

WIDGINA: *(Hanging her head:)* I know. I still feel a little guilty. But you can't think straight with an angry mob chasing you and yelling, "Witch!"

SQUIRE: Well, since you're not dressed like an old hag anymore, I suppose there's more to your story.

SCENE 8

(The forest. Young Widgina 3 enters out of breath.)

WIDGINA: I'd run until I couldn't run anymore. I ended up in a part of the forest I had never been in before. This time at least I had saved up a little money.

(Young Widgina takes off mask and puts it around her basket. She pulls out a bag of coins. From out of nowhere pops up RUMPLESTILTSKIN. Young Widgina is startled.)

SQUIRE: Okay, now she's different again. I'm not even going to try anymore.

WIDGINA: Good. Maybe you can let me finish!

RUMPLESTILTSKIN: Ah, what do we have here? A maiden in distress?

(He tries to grab bag of coins.)

YOUNG WIDGINA: Well, ah, sir... *(Repeatedly moving the bag:)* ...it appears I have just, ah, relocated, and I need to find a house of my own. And a job.

RUMPLESTILTSKIN: *(Giving up on the bag:)* Well, aren't you in luck, my dear? I happen to be the highest rated realtor in the forest! Rumplestiltskin, at your service!

(He takes off hat and bows.)

YOUNG WIDGINA: *(To audience:)* This is lucky...I guess.

RUMPLESTILTSKIN: I have just the place for you! It's a little unconventional, but, ah, yes! That's the charm!

(He peers at her basket and spies the witch mask.)

And I do believe, if I may be so forward, that, perhaps, you are a bit unconventional yourself!

(Young Widgina moves her basket aside.)

SQUIRE: He seems smarmy.

WIDGINA: What do you expect? He was a realtor!

(Rumplestiltskin and Widgina approach a Cookie House.)

YOUNG WIDGINA: It looks like it's made of cookies and candy.

RUMPLESTILTSKIN: That's what makes it so special!

YOUNG WIDGINA: So it can melt in a rainstorm?

RUMPLESTILTSKIN: Sure! You can just whip up a new batch of tasty shingles and some frosting for glue.

YOUNG WIDGINA: It does seem awfully sturdy for gingerbread. How much?

(Rumplestiltskin whispers a number in her ear.)

That seems pretty steep.

RUMPLESTILTSKIN: It's dual zoned! You can also run a bakery from here. It's ideal for someone...such as yourself. *(Looking again at the mask:)* The previous owner found it very useful for luring...I mean, serving the young children from the village nearby. She loved children. *(To audience:)* She always said she could just eat them up! Well, yes or no? I have other clients looking at this place, you know. I don't have all day! I have debts to collect.

YOUNG WIDGINA: What kind of debts?

RUMPLESTILTSKIN: *(Quickly:)* Babies.

YOUNG WIDGINA: Babies?!

RUMPLESTILTSKIN: *(Quickly:)* Rubies! Rubies, my dear.

YOUNG WIDGINA: Oh. Okay—I'll take it.

RUMPLESTILTSKIN: *(Taking out paper:)* Great! Sign here.

(Young Widgina signs. Rumplestiltskin rolls it up and grabs the bag of money before running offstage, giggling.)

SQUIRE: A cookie house?

WIDGINA: Oh, it smelled wonderful! So I moved in and started a bakery.

SQUIRE: When did you learn how to bake?

WIDGINA: I didn't, really. But the previous owner left all her recipes. In fact, it looked like she left in an awful hurry. Anyway, the recipes were fantastic.

(Widgina hands Squire another cookie. Squire eats cookie and nods.)

SCENE 9

(Outside the cottage. Young Widgina is adding more decorations to the outside of the house when a YOUNG MAIDEN comes by, crying. Young Widgina approaches her.)

YOUNG WIDGINA: Are you all right?

MAIDEN: No! My life is ruined!

YOUNG WIDGINA: It can't be that bad. *(Handing her a cookie:)* Here—have a cookie! They're really yummy.

MAIDEN: *(Taking cookie:)* Thanks. But I don't think this is going to help.

YOUNG WIDGINA: What's wrong? You can tell me.

SQUIRE: What are you, Dr. Phil?

WIDGINA: She was obviously upset and needed help. What was I supposed to do?

SQUIRE: With your track record? Leave her alone!

MAIDEN: This creepy little man tricked me into promising him my baby!

YOUNG WIDGINA: Creepy little man?

MAIDEN: Yeah. He had a funny hat and is really obsessed with money! *(To audience:)* He can make straw into gold!

YOUNG WIDGINA: That sounds a lot like my realtor!

MAIDEN: Oh, you know him? Do you remember his name?

YOUNG WIDGINA: It was a really strange name. I can't remember.

MAIDEN: Oh.

(She starts to cry again.)

YOUNG WIDGINA: Wait a minute. He did give me his card.

MAIDEN: His card?

(Young Widgina reaches into her basket and pulls out a card.)

YOUNG WIDGINA: Here it is!

MAIDEN: *(Reading:)*   Rumplestiltskin.   Rumplestiltskin!
Rumplestiltskin!

(Maiden runs offstage, singing the name.)

YOUNG WIDGINA: *(To audience:)* I wonder what that was about? Oh, well, back to house repair.

(Young Widgina returns to fixing the cottage. Lights go down on cottage.)

SQUIRE: Seems like you settled in pretty well.

WIDGINA: Don't be fooled! Trouble was on its way in the form of two obnoxious, little children!

SCENE 10

(Hansel and Gretel walk through the forest, approaching the cottage. Young Widgina 4 is inside the cottage.)

HANSEL: Gretel, I don't think this is a good idea!

GRETEL: Well, we're not going back now!

HANSEL: But I'm getting hungry!

GRETEL: Quit your whining, Hansel! When Mother and Father get back and find out we're not home, they'll be so scared that they'll have to unground us!

HANSEL: If you hadn't shaved the cat we wouldn't be grounded!

GRETEL: *(Pushing Hansel:)* Be quiet! And keep walking. Goldie said that we had to be at the cottage by 3:00!

HANSEL: Why 3:00?

GRETEL: Because that's when the Bears take their walk.

HANSEL: Oh!

(Hansel and Gretel walk around until they reach the cottage.)

Gretel, I'm starving! Please—I need some food!

(Gretel reaches into her bag to find there's a hole. She pokes it dramatically with her finger. Hansel falls to his knees.)

We're gonna die!

GRETEL: *(Checking out the house:)* Hey, check this out!

HANSEL: Food!!

(Hansel runs to the cottage and picks off a big cookie piece. Gretel joins him, a little less enthusiastically. Young Widgina 4 comes out.)

YOUNG WIDGINA: *(Tapping one of them on the shoulder:)* Excuse me!

HANSEL & GRETEL: *(Frightened:)* AHHHH!

SQUIRE: Now, at least she's your size!

(Widgina shoots him an angry glance.)

HANSEL: *(With her mouth full:)* We were starving!

YOUNG WIDGINA: Oh, you poor things! Come on in and have some soup and salad.

HANSEL: But I like cookies!

YOUNG WIDGINA: Hey, where do you live? There's not another house around for miles.

GRETEL: We're from...the village.

HANSEL: Yeah. We got lost because Gretel wanted to run away and make our parents mad. Then we lost all of our food on the way.

(Holds up bag Gretel has been nudging Hansel to be quiet.)

YOUNG WIDGINA: So, why did you run away again?

HANSEL: Gretel was mad because she got grounded for shaving the cat.

GRETEL: *(Hits Hansel:)* What my brother means is that our stepmother...

HANSEL: *(To Gretel:)* We don't have a step...

(Gretel shoves a cookie in Hansel's mouth before he can finish. Young Widgina begins to show Hansel and Gretel into the cottage.)

GRETEL: Our stepmother is very cruel. She tried to beat us, so we had to run away.

(Hansel and Gretel disappear inside the cottage.)

SQUIRE: *(To audience:)* It's always the stepmother!

WIDGINA: I didn't believe her. I figured I'd feed them, then walk them back home before it got too dark.

SQUIRE: But that didn't happen, did it?

WIDGINA: As I said before, no good deed goes unpunished. Apparently, as I was feeding them…and feeding them…and feeding them, their parents had gotten the whole village to set out to look for them. Since Gretel's bag had a hole in it, the food the children had dropped on the way led them all straight to my house.

SCENE 11

(Angry Mob enters, looking around and calling for Hansel and Gretel.)

MOB: This way!
No, that way!
I'm confused! Which way?
Well, why didn't ya say so?

WIDGINA: When I heard the commotion, I went outside and was greeted by a mob of angry villagers!

HANSEL & GRETEL'S FATHER: Have you seen two children?

HANSEL & GRETEL'S MOTHER: A boy and a girl.

YOUNG WIDGINA: Oh, yes. They're in the house having some supper. Are you their parents?

HANSEL & GRETEL'S FATHER: Of course we are! Who else would we be?

(Screams come from Hansel and Gretel from inside the cottage.)

HANSEL: *(Simultaneously)* Get me out of here!
GRETEL: *(Simultaneously)* Help! Help!

(Hansel and Gretel's Mother and Father run up to the cottage door and look inside.)

HANSEL & GRETEL'S MOTHER: He's in the oven!

HANSEL & GRETEL'S FATHER: She put him in the oven!

MOB: She was going to eat them!
She must be a witch!
After her!
Well, why didn't you say so?

(Young Widgina runs offstage followed by the Angry Mob.)

WIDGINA: So that's where we are now. No "Abracadabra."
No "Hocus Pocus." No magic!

SQUIRE: Okay, you've convinced me! You're not a witch.

WIDGINA: Why did you need a witch, anyway?

SQUIRE: *(Pulling out glass slipper:)* Well, the Prince wants me
to find the owner of this shoe. I've looked everywhere! I
thought if you were a witch, you could cast a spell or
something so I could find her.

WIDGINA: *(Checking out the slipper:)* Well, you may be in luck!

SQUIRE: I knew it! You are a witch!

WIDGINA: *(To audience:)* Really? After all this? This one
really needs some help! *(To Squire:)* No! I'm not a witch, but...
(Pulling the other slipper from her basket:) Ta-da!

SQUIRE: Oh! This is great! Now I can take you back to the
castle! You can marry the Prince!

WIDGINA: *(Standing up:)* What? Oh, no! No way! I'm not
marrying any Prince! *(To audience:)* My experience has been
that they aren't too bright, either.

SQUIRE: But you're the owner of the shoe!

WIDGINA: Well, technically, yes, but I've never been to the
castle.

SQUIRE: What? What do you mean?

WIDGINA: See, I loaned my shoes to a girl who came by my
bakery looking to buy bread.

SQUIRE: Oh, I see. She came to buy bread and you gave her
shoes!

WIDGINA: She was a silly girl. Here—I'm tired of telling
stories. Let me just show you!

SCENE 12

(Widgina leaves bench and passes to the middle of the stage and into the cottage. Cinderella enters, comes up to the cottage, breaks off a piece and starts to eat it.)

WIDGINA: *(Coming out:)* May I ask what you're doing?

CINDERELLA: *(Startled:)* Oh! Well, you see...

WIDGINA: Spit it out, girl! I don't have all day!

CINDERELLA: *(Aside, to Widgina:)* I don't remember you being this rude to me.

WIDGINA: Sorry. I'm just getting tired of all this storytelling! Let's try again. How can I help you, miss?

CINDERELLA: Well, you see, I want to go to the Prince's ball tonight, but I don't have my chores finished, and I need some bread for supper.

WIDGINA: If you needed bread, why were you taking apart my wall?

CINDERELLA: *(Sheepishly:)* I thought it might make a good dessert.

(Widgina reaches into her basket and hands Cinderella some bread.)

WIDGINA: This should take care of it.

CINDERELLA: Oh, thank you!

WIDGINA: *(Looking down:)* Oh, but are those the shoes you're wearing?

CINDERELLA: *(Looking embarrassed:)* They're the only ones I have!

WIDGINA: Wait a second.

(She goes into the cottage and emerges with a pair of shoes.)

WIDGINA: I got these in payment once from a really hungry fairy. Pretty, aren't they?

CINDERELLA: Oh, they're beautiful!   *(Taking shoes:)* Thank you!

(She runs off.)

WIDGINA: Hey — don't forget to bring them back!

(Widgina returns to the bench with the Squire. Lights out on the cottage.)

SQUIRE: So how did you end up with only one shoe?

WIDGINA: I don't know what that girl did at the ball, but when she came by the next day, she only had one shoe!

SQUIRE: Do you know where she lives?

WIDGINA: No, but she'll probably come back to my bakery soon. She really did want to try some dessert!

SQUIRE: Great! Let's go! I want to be there when she comes back!

SCENE 13

(The Squire and Widgina cross to the cottage. Everyone is there, eating pieces from the house.)

SQUIRE: I didn't know there was going to be a party!

WIDGINA: Neither did I. Hey! Stop eating my house!

(No one responds.)

HEY!! I said, stop eating my house!!

(Everyone stops suddenly.)

What are you all doing here?

RAPUNZEL: Oh, Widgina! We've been looking for you ever so long!

SNOW WHITE: It just wasn't the same since you ran away! After the Prince, um, revived me, I came looking for you.

WIDGINA: *(To audience:)* Wasn't I right here just a minute ago? Where were they looking? *(To everyone:)* Do I need to get out my running shoes again?

HANSEL & GRETEL'S MOTHER: *(Holding Hansel & Gretel by the ears:)* Oh, no. The children finally told us what really happened!

RAPUNZEL: I tried to tell them, too...but then I got distracted.

(Cinderella enters.)

CINDERELLA: Oh, good—you're here! I still haven't been able to find the other shoe.

SQUIRE: It's here, my lady!

CINDERELLA: Oh! Good!

(Widgina pushes Cinderella toward the Squire.)

WIDGINA: And here's your girl! She's the one who wore the shoes!

SQUIRE: My lady, the Prince has sent me to find you! He requests your hand in marriage!

(Prince enters.)

PRINCE: That is correct, my fairest! I entreat you—would you be my wife?

CINDERELLA: What?!

SNOW WHITE & RAPUNZEL: *(Stepping out front, together:)* WHAT?!

PRINCE: *(Hiding behind Squire:)* Oh, um…ladies! You're here!

RAPUNZEL: My Prince!

SNOW WHITE: YOUR Prince? He's MY Prince!

CINDERELLA: Um, didn't he just propose to me?

RAPUNZEL: Yeah, after proposing to me!

SNOW WHITE: And me!

(Cinderella, Snow White and Rapunzel come together and direct an icy stare at the Prince. They walk purposefully toward him as he backs away, staying behind the Squire.)

WIDGINA: *(To audience:)* This is even better than the predicaments I usually get myself in!

PRINCE: Squire, tell them something!

SQUIRE: *(Moving away from the Prince:)* Um, I think you're on your own!

PRINCE: *(Standing upright:)* Then I bid you all adieu!

(Prince runs offstage, followed by Rapunzel, Snow White and Cinderella.)

SQUIRE: Wow, I knew he was corny, but I didn't know he was such a jerk!

WIDGINA: I told you — not much going on upstairs.

SQUIRE: Well, looks like I'm out of a job.

HANSEL: These shingles are really delicious!

GRETEL: Yeah, and the shutters are to die for!

RED: Granny needs some of these recipes!

RUMPLESTILTSKIN: *(To Widgina:)* Young lady, if you sell me back this property, I can double your return! This is a gold mine!

> *(Widgina looks around her at all the people enjoying her baked goods.)*

WIDGINA: Well, it certainly looks like this bakery fills a niche in this forest. Maybe I'll try and give it a go.

HANSEL: Yeah! Hey, everyone! All the free desserts you can eat!

> *(Everyone cheers and continues eating.)*

WIDGINA: *(To Squire:)* Looks like I'm going to need some security around here. You want a job?

SQUIRE: Sure! Beats fending off jilted maidens! Besides — there's never a dull moment around here! But what are we gonna do about all these trespassers?

> *(Widgina turns to the audience and waves her hand over her basket. She pulls out a handful of cookies.)*

WIDGINA: Cookies! Free cookies!

EVERYONE: Cookies! Cookies!
Where? Which way?

Over there! She's got them!
Well, why didn't you say so?

(Everyone moves away from Widgina after grabbing a cookie.)

WIDGINA: (Shrugging shoulders to audience:) So I used some literary license!

(Lights out. Curtain call follows. The End.)

The Author Speaks

What inspired you to write this play?
I've always enjoyed fairy tales—the magic, the princesses, the frogs. I was inspired to write this play while searching through other plays for my husband's middle school to perform. The plays we looked at seemed either dated or hokey. When we couldn't find what we were looking for, I decided to write one myself. I had often thought about writing a play that would incorporate different fairy tales. I was intrigued by the idea of several misunderstandings causing the heroine of the story to be viewed as a witch.

Was the structure of the play influenced by any other work?
I drew on several works to create the play. While the play's structure is not based on any specific work, the idea to incorporate several fairy tale characters was inspired by the musical, *Into the Woods*. The fast-paced, witty dialogue was influenced by comedies such as *The Importance of Being Earnest*. Having Widgina and the Squire narrate the story is similar to a successful play we performed called *The Somewhat True Tale of Robin Hood*.

Have you dealt with the same theme in other works that you have written?
This is my first play, but the theme of "things are not always as they appear," so "do not be quick to judge" is also the theme of several of the children's books I have written that have yet to be published.

What do you hope to achieve with this work?
I think theatre is a great experience for young people: it gives them self-confidence, teaches them how to work in groups, and gives them a place to belong. I love working with young

people, and I would hope that those performing this play would develop a love for theatre arts while learning something about stage work. For those who watch the play, I would hope that they would be entertained, and take to heart that we should not judge people on surface appearances, and that there are always two sides to each story.

What inspired you to become a playwright?
I have always loved writing. Being able to put into words all the ideas roaming around in my brain was fun for me in school. My fifth grade English teacher was amazing; she had us write all the time. She was very encouraging and told me I should be a writer. I have been writing ever since. I was drawn to the theatre in high school where I caught the acting bug. Writing for the stage now allows me to combine the passions I have for writing and the stage. I love developing characters and fleshing out their personalities, as well as figuring out the action on the stage.

How did you research the subject?
For this play, I read through several fairy tales to decide which ones would work best in the story. I decided Widgina would be the same throughout the story, so I read all the fairy tales with a witch as the antagonist.

Shakespeare gave advice to the players in *Hamlet*; if you could give advice to your cast what would it be?
I would say "enjoy yourself." Learn the lines early so you can use your entire body to act during rehearsals. This is such a fun play that the audience will be transported to the woods with all of you!

How was the first production different from the vision that you created in your mind?
As this was my first play, I wasn't sure what I expected. The cast seemed to enjoy playing the characters as much as I enjoyed creating them. I wrote it with simple staging in mind, which worked well with our middle school actors. The set and costumes brought the production to life. Since I was able to be part of the direction from start to finish, the end result was extremely close to my vision.

About the Author

Cheryl Hadley is a wife and mother of two. Cheryl loves writing, and has written plays, skits, books of poetry, children's books, various curriculum for children's ministries, and many other types of material. She has worked as a substitute teacher, residential child care worker, and day care provider, while raising children and supporting her husband Keith's job teaching choir and drama at a local public school. She continues to assist him in directing school dramatic productions.

About YouthPLAYS

YouthPLAYS (www.youthplays.com) is a publisher of award-winning professional dramatists and talented new discoveries, each with an original theatrical voice, and all dedicated to expanding the vocabulary of theatre for young actors and audiences. On our website you'll find one-act and full-length plays and musicals for teen and pre-teen (and even college) actors, as well as duets and monologues for competition. Many of our authors' works have been widely produced at high schools and middle schools, youth theatres and other TYA companies, both amateur and professional, as well as at elementary schools, camps, churches and other institutions serving young audiences and/or actors worldwide. Most are intended for performance by young people, while some are intended for adult actors performing for young audiences.

YouthPLAYS was co-founded by professional playwrights Jonathan Dorf and Ed Shockley. It began merely as an additional outlet to market their own works, which included a substantial body of award-winning published and unpublished plays and musicals. Those interested in their published plays were directed to the respective publishers'· websites, and unpublished plays were made available in electronic form. But when they saw the desperate need for material for young actors and audiences—coupled with their experience that numerous quality plays for young people weren't finding a home—they made the decision to represent the work of other playwrights as well. Dozens and dozens of authors are now members of the YouthPLAYS family, with scripts available both electronically and in traditional acting editions. We continue to grow as we look for exciting and challenging plays and musicals for young actors and audiences.

About ProduceaPlay.com

Let's put up a play! Great idea! But producing a play takes time, energy and knowledge. While finding the necessary time and energy is up to you, ProduceaPlay.com is a website designed to assist you with that third element: knowledge.

Created by YouthPLAYS' co-founders, Jonathan Dorf and Ed Shockley, ProduceaPlay.com serves as a resource for producers at all levels as it addresses the many facets of production. As Dorf and Shockley speak from their years of experience (as playwrights, producers, directors and more), they are joined by a group of award-winning theatre professionals and experienced teachers from the world of academic theatre, all making their expertise available for free in the hope of helping this and future generations of producers, whether it's at the school or university level, or in community or professional theatres.

The site is organized into a series of major topics, each of which has its own page that delves into the subject in detail, offering suggestions and links for further information. For example, Publicity covers everything from Publicizing Auditions to How to Use Social Media to Posters to whether it's worth hiring a publicist. Casting details Where to Find the Actors, How to Evaluate a Resume, Callbacks and even Dealing with Problem Actors. You'll find guidance on your Production Timeline, The Theater Space, Picking a Play, Budget, Contracts, Rehearsing the Play, The Program, House Management, Backstage, and many other important subjects.

The site is constantly under construction, so visit often for the latest insights on play producing, and let it help make your play production dreams a reality.

More from YouthPLAYS

Brave Little Tailor by Randy Wyatt

Comedy. 40-60 minutes. 2-20+ males, 2-20+ females (13-30 performers possible).

When Chris climbs into his Grandmother's attic and blows upon a magic ocarina, the mysterious Storyteller and his many spirits and elves appear. But Chris is in for a surprise when the Storyteller sends Chris (and his trusty cat Keara) into the fable as the little tailor himself! Chris doesn't feel very brave to begin with, but once he encounters a not-so-bright giant, the royal court, two vain dragons, a mysterious unicorn and the dreaded Swamp Monster, perhaps he'll learn where bravery comes from in this comic adventure for young audiences.

Crimes and Rhymes by James Grob

Comedy. 55-65 minutes, 5 males, 5 females, 5 either (with some flexibility).

When Mother Goose is missing and The Big Bad Wolf is the main suspect, the President of the United States sends his top special agent to Storyland to help solve the mystery. Can a host of characters from well-known nursery rhymes and fairy tales help the special agent and the local sheriff get to the bottom of things?

Clay by Carol S. Lashof

Dramedy. 30-40 minutes. 2 males, 2 females.

Aaron, Zeta and Will are as different as three students could be. One works tirelessly yet struggles to pass. One excels by cutting every corner, and one attends school intermittently despite exceptional intelligence and creativity. Forced to interact by a group assignment, they confront themselves, each other and the magic of molding clay.

The Christmas Princess by Arthur M. Jolly

Fairy Tale. 60-80 minutes (flexible). 4-5+ males, 4-8+ females (8-25 performers possible, including a size and gender-flexible ensemble of dancers).

It's Christmas Eve—and the palace is in turmoil. The next day is not only Christmas, but the wedding day of the beautiful (but spoiled) Princess and the handsome (but dumb as a bag of rocks) Prince Valiant. The problem: the Princess doesn't want to marry a stupid prince. Desperate to find a way out of the marriage, she seeks the advice of Watt the Witch, who sends her on a quest to find three magical gifts that will allow her to escape her wedding.

Dodge by Ed Shockley

Comedy. 25-35 minutes. 6-15 males, 5-15 females (11-30 performers possible).

Dodge disappears after being sent to fetch more gold paint. She's really just trying to avoid the work of painting the leaves for autumn, but the other Elves assume that she has been waylaid by the winter Gnomes—and now war is brewing. Holmstead, a character worthy of Arthur Conan Doyle, sets out with Swallow, following the clues the hapless Dodge has left behind, as Dodge tries desperately to think of a way to return and avert war without revealing her laziness and deception.

The Hanging of the Greens by Claudia Haas

Young Audiences. 60-70 minutes. 3 males, 8 females, 9 either (20 performers total).

There is a legend that wreaths, swags and garlands must hang on every doorway or window before the arrival of winter. This will protect the home from Pinella the Witch who seeks to steal little children and make them her slaves. But what happens when the children in one home decide to play and dream and shirk their responsibilities? They are ripe to be kidnapped by Pinella!

Herby Alice Counts Down to Yesterday by Nicole B. Adkins

Comedy. 45-50 minutes. 3-7 males, 3-7 females, 4-20+ either (10-50+ performers possible).

Middle school rocket scientist Herby Alice has ambitions as big as the universe, and no time for interviews. Rose Plum, media hopeful, needs a juicy story to get in good with the school broadcast elite. How far is she willing to go to be a star? Or will mad scientists, aliens, befuddled teachers, demanding executives, and the space-time continuum overrun the show?

Miracle in Mudville by D.W. Gregory

Comedy. 60-70 minutes. 5-11+ males, 13-17+ females (21-31+ performers possible).

Casey is the worst ballplayer in the Mudville Little League, the butt of jokes and an embarrassment to his Dad, who brags of his glory days in the outfield. But he's not alone in feeling inadequate; his friends suffer by comparison to their parents, too. Then a chance encounter with the ghost of the town's dead librarian throws Casey and his friends into a time warp—where they discover that some of their parents' big adventures didn't quite happen the way they said...

Telling William Tell by Evan Guilford-Blake

Dramedy. 80-85 minutes. 7-11 males, 4-10 females (11-21 performers possible).

The children grab the spotlight in this retelling of the story of the mythical Swiss hero—famed for shooting an apple off his son's head—framed by a fictionalized story of Rossini writing his famed opera. Music by the great composer enriches this thrilling tale of Switzerland's fight for freedom and the birth of a new work of musical art.